MAKING CONTACT!

MARCONI GOES WIRELESS

Monica Kulling   *Illustrated by Richard Rudnicki*

TUNDRA BOOKS

For my brother Edwin,
remembering our radio days
M.K.

For my brother Stephen,
the electrical engineer in the family
R.R.

Special thanks to Henry M. Bradford of Wolfville, Nova Scotia, historian on wireless telegraphy, for generously reading the manuscript, and to Richard Rudnicki for introducing me to Henry. – M.K.

Thanks to Henry M. Bradford for technical support and to Monica Kulling for help with research. Thanks to all my models: Wesley Rimmington, Bob Johnston, Scott Riker, Anthony Kuhn, Darielle Rudnicki, Andrea, Alexander, and Erica Hilchie Pye, Tim Tracey, Charlie Bourne, John Fraser, Matt Andrea, Kyle Jackson, Kevin Robins, and James and Diana Hazelton. And a special thanks to Susan Tooke. – R.R.

Paperback edition published by Tundra Books, 2016

Text copyright © 2013 by Monica Kulling
Illustrations copyright © 2013 by Richard Rudnicki

Tundra Books, a division of Random House of Canada Limited, a Penguin Random House Company

Library and Archives Canada Cataloguing in Publication

Kulling, Monica, 1952-, author
    Making contact! : Marconi goes wireless / Monica Kulling ; illustrated by Richard Rudnicki.

(Great idea series)
Originally published: Toronto, Ontario : Tundra Books, ©2013.
Includes bibliographical references.
ISBN 978-1-101-91842-5 (paperback)

    1. Marconi, Guglielmo, 1874-1937. 2. Inventors – Italy – Biography – Juvenile literature. 3. Radio – History – Juvenile literature. 4. Telegraph, Wireless – Marconi system – History – Juvenile literature. I. Rudnicki, Richard, illustrator II. Title. III. Series: Great idea series

TK5739.M37K85 2016   j621.384092   C2015-904004-3

Published simultaneously in the United States of America by Tundra Books of Northern New York, a division of Random House of Canada Limited, a Penguin Random House Company

Library of Congress Control Number: 2012947610

Sources of Inspiration:

Sonneborn, Liz. Great Life Stories: Guglielmo Marconi: Inventor of Wireless Technology. New York: Franklin Watts, 2005.

Weightman, Gavin. Signor Marconi's Magic Box. London: HarperCollins Publishers, 2003.

Zannos, Susan. Guglielmo Marconi and the Story of Radio Waves. Delaware: Mitchell Lane Publishers, 2005.

Internet: www.factmonster.com/biography/var/guglielmomarconi.html

Edited by Sue Tate
Designed by Leah Springate
The artwork in this book was rendered in acrylic on 300 lb. hot press watercolor paper.
Printed and bound in China

www.penguinrandomhouse.ca

1 2 3 4 5   20 19 18 17 16

Radio Days

There was a time
all round the world
when Radio was queen.
She waited grandly
in the room
for her subjects
to gather at her feet.
"Give me your ears.
Listen," she said.

So we sat quietly,
hearing stories
that took us to other worlds;
listening to the sounds
of horses' hooves,
block hitting block –
Clip-clop. Clip-clop.

We did nothing but listen.
Imagine.

The storm pelted Benjamin Franklin as he flew his kite on the hill. A lightning bolt struck the wet string and zapped down to the iron key tied at the end. The charge then jolted into a jar designed to store electricity.

As a boy, Guglielmo (*Goo-le-EL-mo*) Marconi loved science and invention. His hero was Benjamin Franklin, who'd flown a kite in a storm to prove that lightning is a charge of electricity.

"There is energy in the air!" announced Marconi excitedly.

Marconi was born in 1874 in Bologna, Italy, the younger of two sons of Annie and Giuseppe Marconi. His wealthy family owned a home in the city and a villa in the countryside. *Villa Griffone* was in Pontecchio, near Bologna.

When the baby Marconi was brought to the villa, the gardener said, "What big ears he has."

"He will be able to hear the still, small voices in the air," replied Signora Marconi proudly.

These words held a seed of truth, for Guglielmo Marconi would grow up to become the father of wireless communication.

Marconi did not do well in school, so his family hired tutors. By age ten, he was reading the books in his father's library.

The German scientist Heinrich Hertz wrote about radio waves. He produced them by using a high-voltage electric spark. Marconi was fascinated. He learned Morse code, the language of the telegraph. A retired telegraph operator taught him how to tap messages on the telegraph machine.

In 1894, when Marconi was twenty,
he and his brother, Alfonso, went on
vacation to the Alps, in northern Italy.
One night, while trying to fall asleep,
Marconi was struck by the spark of a
great idea. Could *he* find a way to use
radio waves to send wireless messages?

It had never been done before. Marconi
would have to act fast if he wanted to be
the first.

Marconi was a born inventor. He could concentrate for hours, and, when an experiment failed, he simply started over. But an inventor needed equipment and a place to work.

"We will clear out two attic rooms at *Villa Griffone*," said his mother. She was almost as excited as her son.

"Inventing is a fine hobby," said his father. "But how will you make a living?"

Despite his doubts, Marconi's father gave him money to buy equipment.

Marconi experimented with batteries, antennas, and an electric spark generator. He would be successful if he could send a radio wave signal to the receiver on the other side of the room.

Then one day, in the late summer of 1895, Marconi tapped the telegraph key and the bell on the receiver rang.

"It works!" he told his mother. "The signal is going through the air without wires!"

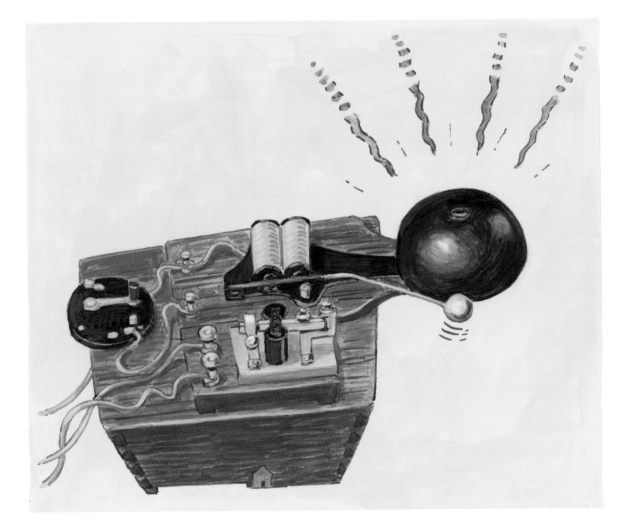

It was time to test the wireless telegraph over a longer distance. Alfonso and two assistants carried the antennas and receiving equipment more than a mile from the villa over a hill. They brought along a hunting rifle. If the signal from the telegraph came through, they would fire a single shot.

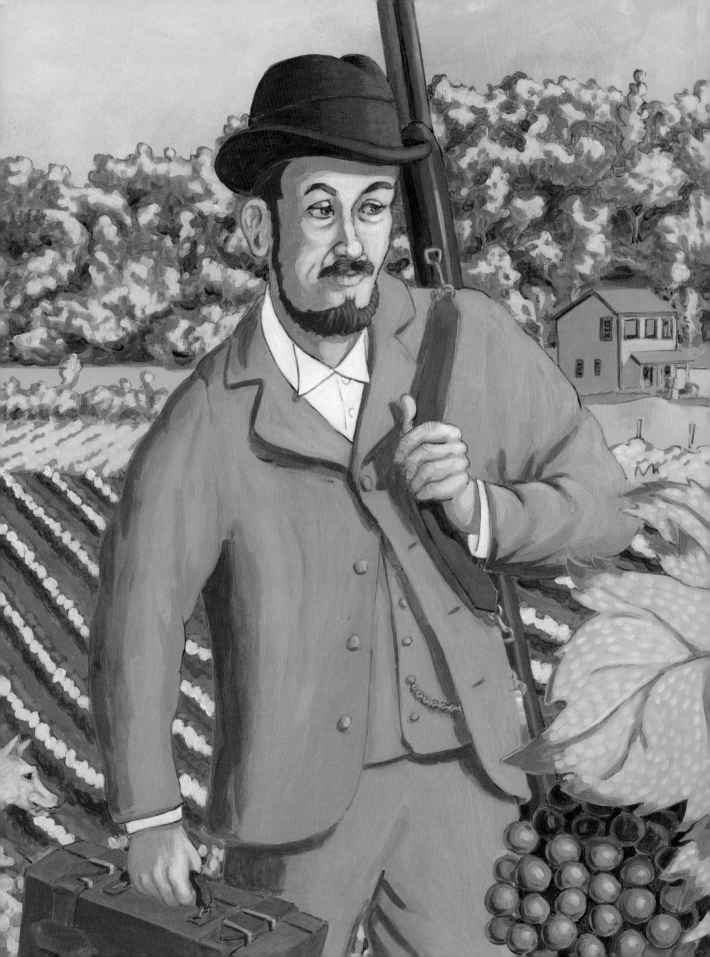

Marconi sat at a table under a tree with the wireless transmitter. He pressed the key three times. Then he waited.

Marconi was certain that radio waves could travel great distances. Mountains or the curve of the earth would not stand in their way. This was the final test of his idea.

Suddenly a gunshot rang out. The signal had been received!

At the age of twenty-one, Marconi had invented a working wireless telegraph.

His Irish mother, Annie, had many relatives in England. In 1896, Annie and Marconi traveled there to show off his invention. When they arrived in London, Annie's nephew Henry Jameson-Davis met them at the train station.

"You need a patent," he told Marconi straight off.

So Marconi filed a patent to protect his wireless telegraph from being copied.

In England, Marconi gave many astonishing demonstrations of his wireless telegraph. One of the most exciting involved Queen Victoria.

The queen's son Albert was recovering from a knee injury on the royal yacht, several miles out to sea. She asked Marconi to set up a wireless telegraph, both at her summer home and on the yacht, so that she could get daily updates on her son's recovery. No one had ever before sent messages from land to a ship at sea or from a ship to land.

Soon Marconi was sending telegrams from the yacht to the summerhouse. Queen Victoria marveled at this new invention.

The success of Marconi's ship-to-shore messages encouraged him to try to send a signal across the immense Atlantic Ocean. He chose Poldhu Point in Cornwall, England, to build his transmitting station.

The first transmitting antenna Marconi built did not last long. Fierce winds tore it apart. The next antenna was fan-shaped and stood 210 feet (64 meters) high. The transmitter needed to be powerful enough for the Morse code taps to be heard over 2000 miles (3218 kilometers) away – on the other side of the Atlantic!

On Signal Hill in St. John's, Newfoundland, Marconi and his assistants set themselves up in an old military hospital. It was winter, and an icy wind blasted the hill.

Marconi used balloons and kites to get his antenna high into the sky. He was flying a kite in a storm, just like his hero Benjamin Franklin!

The Poldhu Point crew sent the Morse code signal for the letter *S* for three hours every day. Marconi listened patiently for the signal through an earpiece, but heard nothing. As the days went by, he grew more and more discouraged.

Finally, on December 12, 1901, Marconi heard three clicks on the receiver. Excitedly, he handed the earpiece to an assistant, who also heard three clicks. The signal was scratchy and faint, but Marconi and his assistant could hear it. Marconi had made contact!

For the first time ever, a wireless signal had traveled the distance between two continents. It was only the beginning.

Save Our Ship!

Over one hundred years ago, the "unsinkable" *Titanic* hit an iceberg and sank on April 15, 1912. There were only 705 survivors out of more than 2200 passengers and crew.

Marconi's wireless telegraph was both a blessing and a curse on that voyage. The *Titanic* received six ice warnings on the day of the collision, but these were ignored. The passengers had been tying up the telegraph with greetings from the middle of the ocean.

The last telegraph sent from the *Titanic* stated: "We are sinking fast, passengers being put into boats."

If not for Marconi's invention, the ship named the *Carpathia* would not have heard the call for help or been able to race to the rescue and locate the survivors. No one would have lived to tell the story.

Things to spot

James and Cath enjoy exploring. They are looking forward to spotting some of the rare things that can only be found in Puzzle Jungle. There is something to look out for on every double page.

blue donut stone

carved pole

giant butterfly

yellow spider

uppa gum tree

green monkey

pink palm

red string plant

mini-anteater

stripy giraffe

swampy snake

spotty bug

green tiger

Marcy

Marcy lives in Puzzle Jungle. She is going to enter the kite competition, even though she isn't a child! Marcy has a sneaky plan. Find out what she is up to as you read this book. Watch out for her on almost every double page.

Kite competitors

The kite competition is taking place on Bungi Beach, which lies at the very edge of Puzzle Jungle. Some children are already making their way there. Can you spot a child with a kite on almost every double page?

3

Max's house

On Friday, James and Cath arrived in Puzzle Jungle for the kite competition. They were looking forward to staying with their friend Max, who lived in a house high in the tree tops. The way to Max's front door was exciting, but tricky. James and Cath would have to climb vines and ladders and clamber across tree trunks to reach it.

Can you find the safe route up to Max's house?

A strange story

"Hello," Max said, as James and Cath bounded through the door. "You're here at last. I was just making you a welcome snack in the kitchen when I heard noises. I rushed out and saw Marcy sneaking away with my grandad's old map. Marcy wants to win the kite competition and I think I know her plan."

James and Cath were puzzled, so Max explained.

Grandad was a bird watcher. His greatest discovery was . . .

. . . the Soaraway bird. It can fly higher than anything in the world.

It lives on an island in the middle of a swamp, deep in Puzzle Jungle.

My grandad's map shows where this island is.

Marcy plans to find the island and steal a feather from the Soaraway bird.

She'll fasten it to her kite and it will fly high and win the competition!

"There is only one Soaraway bird left in the world," Max continued. "We can't let Marcy harm it. She may have the map, but I have written all I know about the island in my blue and red diary with the yellow triangle on the front."

Can you find Max's diary?

The trail begins

James opened the diary. Sure enough, Max had written notes and drawn pictures showing the start of the trail to the island where the Soaraway bird lived.

"There's no time to lose," said Max. "Marcy already has a head start. We must stop her."

The three friends scrambled down to the jungle below.

"Which way now?" Cath asked.

This way to the island

MY MAP SHOWING START OF TRAIL TO THE ISLAND.

Notes
The Soaraway bird lives on a fantastic island in a swamp somewhere deep in Puzzle Jungle. The island is always covered in purple mist.

8

Max looked at the map in his diary. He had marked the path they must take first, but how did it match up with the real jungle paths they could see in front of them?

Can you see which path they must take?

Sleepy sloths

James, Cath and Max ran up the path, past a herd of partying elephants and into a clearing. Here they found a group of strange looking animals. They were sloths and they were very angry.

"That elephants' party is keeping us awake!" cried the sloths. "We can't sleep with all this noise. Will you help us to find new branches to hang from?"

Max led the sloths far away from the elephants. Then James and Cath listened in amazement as the sloths actually told them what kind of branches each of them liked to hang from. Soon the children had found all of the right branches for all of the sloths.

Can you find the right branches for all of the sloths to hang from?

A fruity problem

"The Soaraway bird is sleepy, too!" cried the sloths as the children waved goodbye. They ran on until they came to a market place.

"Let's buy a piece of fruit each," said James.

"Good idea," said Max. "But red fruit gives me a rash."

"Me too," said Cath. "And James and I don't like green fruit. We only have fifteen puzzle pennies between us and I want to buy a bead bracelet as well."

What fruit, and which bracelet, should they choose?

Fabric
20pp

FRUIT

FRUIT

purple juicy fruits 5pp each

orange ovals 6pp each

yellow belly 4pp each

bananas 5pp each

purple plum-lovelys 7pp each

grab-a-grapes 7pp each

ugli-bugli fruit 5pp each

strawjelly berries 4pp each

Jungle animals

Munching on the fruit, the three explorers journeyed on. Suddenly Max stopped short. Ahead was a maze of paths.

"There are deadly jungle animals all around us," Max whispered. "We must be careful not to take a path alongside a lion, a tiger, a snake, a leopard, a giant gorilla, or an alligator."

Cath and James looked around. They couldn't see any animals, so they followed Max closely.

Can you find a safe route along the paths to the bridge?

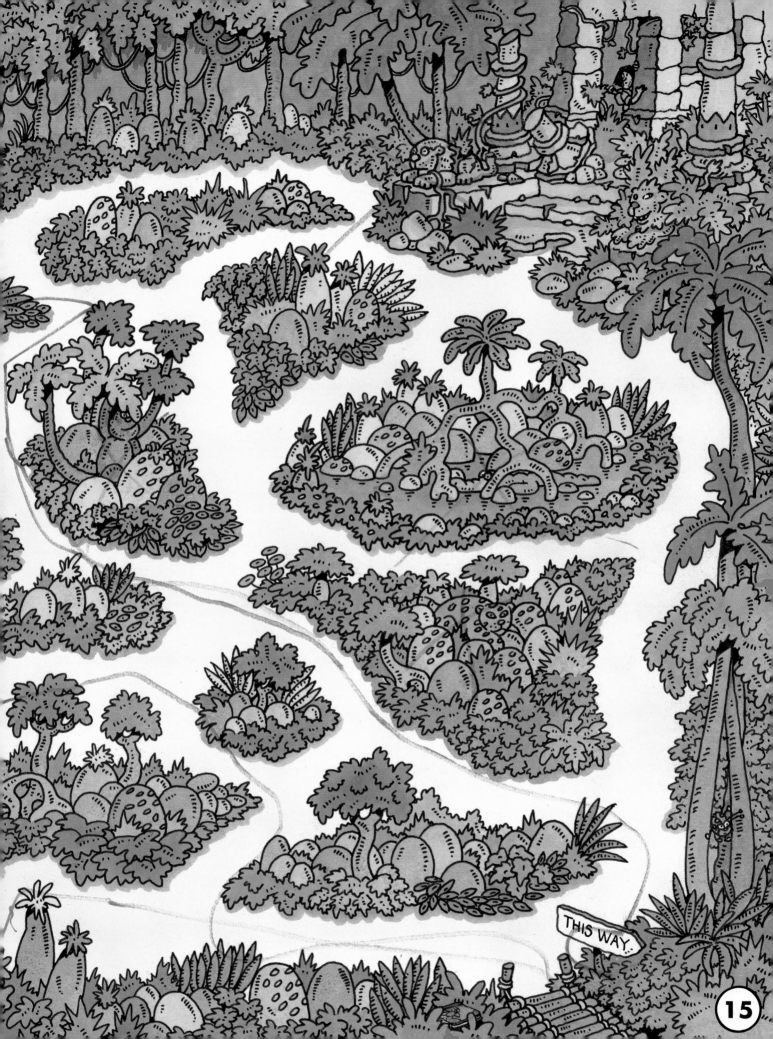

THIS WAY

15

Monkey business

The children ran safely across the bridge. Soon they found themselves in a strange, rocky place. They were just wondering which way to go next when they saw a man.

"We're looking for the island where the Soaraway bird lives," said Max.

"The golden feathered Soaraway, eh?" said the man. "Well, I'm studying the monkeys of Puzzle Jungle. If you can help me find five black mini-monkeys, three brown gibbons, two blue baboons and an orange orang-utan, I will give you my magic compass. Follow it north and you will find the island. I'd go myself, but I have too much monkey studying to do."

Can you find all the monkeys?

Hello, I'm Monty, the monkey man.

Jungle journey

The man thanked the children for finding the monkeys and gave them the magic compass.

"One more thing," he called after them. "If the compass fails to work, look for the red tree that points the way!"

Max set the compass for north and they set off, deeper into Puzzle Jungle.

They waded through marshes ...

...and crawled under waterfalls.

They crossed a swaying bridge.

They climbed up a mountain...

...and down the other side.

They came to a stop at some sludgy sand. Max leaned down for a closer look and stumbled over a tree trunk. The compass fell from his hand. He grabbed for it, but too late! The compass sank without a trace. Which way should they go now?

Do you know?

Raft Craft

They followed the arrow on the red tree until they came to a small beach. Max looked across the murky, swampy water.

"That misty purple island's the one we're looking for!" he cried.

"We'll have to build a raft to get there," said Cath. "My jungle survival book will show us how."

She flipped to the page on useful rafts while James and Max scouted around for materials.

Which raft should they make? Can you find all the materials?

Jungle Survival
Useful Rafts

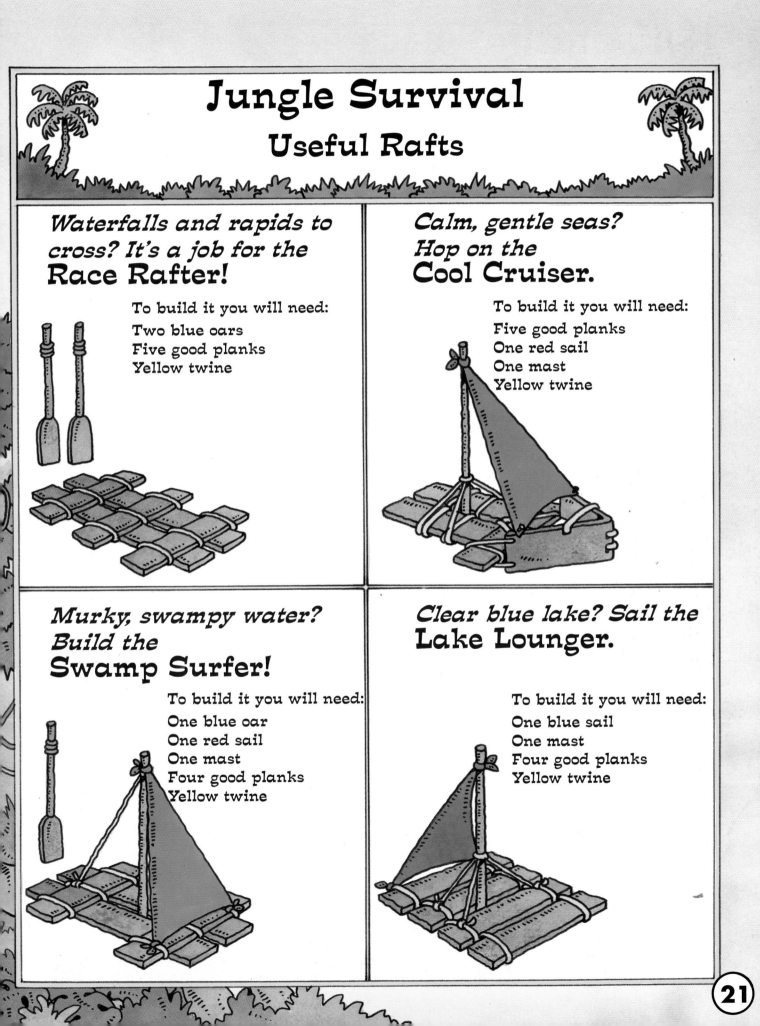

Waterfalls and rapids to cross? It's a job for the
Race Rafter!

To build it you will need:

Two blue oars
Five good planks
Yellow twine

Calm, gentle seas? Hop on the
Cool Cruiser.

To build it you will need:

Five good planks
One red sail
One mast
Yellow twine

Murky, swampy water? Build the
Swamp Surfer!

To build it you will need:

One blue oar
One red sail
One mast
Four good planks
Yellow twine

Clear blue lake? Sail the
Lake Lounger.

To build it you will need:

One blue sail
One mast
Four good planks
Yellow twine

An amazing place

The Swamp Surfer wobbled across the water and reached the island safely. But as the three explorers jumped off, it sank!

They squelched to the shore and gasped with amazement. Strange looking plants and trees grew all around, and there were birds too. Was the Soaraway bird here? Did it really exist?

James, Cath and Max thought back to all they had found out about the Soaraway bird. They knew there was only one in the world, it was sleepy and it had golden feathers. Then they saw it!

Can you find the Soaraway bird?

Caught!

The three adventurers gazed in silent wonder at the snoozing creature. Could this really be the amazing high-flying Soaraway bird?

"I think we got here before Marcy did," said Max. "But perhaps we should make sure she isn't sneaking around somewhere."

The Soaraway bird woke up. He was startled, and so was Marcy.

Squawk

The Soaraway bird flew away to safety, and Marcy fell back with surprise. She landed – SPLAT – in a hole.

"Follow me," said Cath. "Our raft may have sunk, but I saw something else we can use to sail away in."

What has Cath spotted?

Escape!

Cath had spotted Marcy's boat! They scrambled aboard and pushed off from the shore.

"Where to now, Max?" Cath asked.

"If we hurry," said Max, "we might just be in time for the kite flying competition on Bungi Beach."

James laughed and clapped his hands. "And I can see where the competition is," he cried. "Look there's a kite!"

Can you see it?

Kite flying

Max, James and Cath splashed through the shallow water onto the sandy beach and ran to join the competition. The sky was filled with wonderful kites.

"We're just in time," Max panted. "I bet my kite flies the highest."

James and Cath looked up at the sky and grinned.

"Sorry Max," they called. "We don't think you'll beat the highest flier of them all!"

What have Cath and James spotted? Do you recognize anyone else here?

JUDGES

Later on

Max, Cath and James did win something in the competition – a trophy for being the most adventurous kite flyers!

Later that day, as they sat on Max's balcony, Cath asked "What are all the things on the blanket, Max?"

Max grinned. "My grandad may have been a great explorer, but he was also forgetful. These are the things he dropped on his journey to find the Soaraway bird. I picked them up along the way. They must have been lying in the jungle for ages."

Whee!

Why not look back carefully through the book and see if you can spot all of Grandad's things?

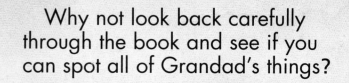

Answers

Pages 4-5
Max's house

The safe route to Max's house is shown in black.

Pages 6-7
A strange story

Max's diary is here.

Pages 8-9
The trail begins

They must take this path. It is the only one that matches Max's drawing.

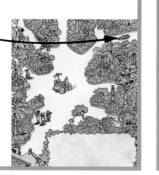

Pages 10-11
Sleepy sloths

Match the letters to find which sloths can hang where.

Pages 12-13
A fruity problem

Cath buys a bead bracelet for 3pp (puzzle pennies). She buys a Yellow Belly fruit for 4pp. James buys a Strawjelly berry for 4pp and Max buys an Apple Surprise for 4pp.
That adds up to 15pp exactly.

Pages 14-15
Jungle animals

The safe route along the paths is marked in black. The hidden animals are circled in red.

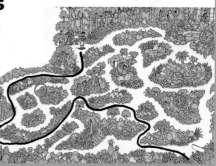

Pages 16-17
Monkey business

The monkeys are circled in black.

Pages 18-19
Jungle journey

They must follow the arrow on this red tree.

Pages 20-21
Raft craft

The water is murky and swampy, so they should build the Swamp Surfer. The materials they will need are circled in black.

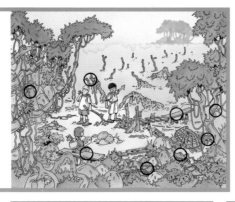

Pages 22-23
An amazing place

The Soaraway bird is here.

Pages 24-25
Caught!

Cath has spotted a boat. It is Marcy's. Here it is.

Pages 26-27
Escape!

The kite is here. This is Bungi Beach.

Pages 28-29 Kite flying

Cath and James have spotted Marcy. Here she is being carried away by the Soaraway bird!

Did you spot everything?
Jungle objects

Grandad's things

Kite competitors

Did you remember to find one rare jungle object on every double page? And did you look back through the book and spot all of Grandad's things?

Pages	Jungle objects	Grandad's things
4-5	swampy snake	pocket watch
6-7	carved pole	binoculars
8-9	yellow spider	knife
10-11	mini-anteater	forked stick
12-13	stripy giraffe	hat
14-15	spotty bug	book
16-17	green tiger	magnifying glass
18-19	green monkey	spotty handkerchief
20-21	blue donut stone	drinking flask
22-23	uppa gum tree	glasses
24-25	red string plant	boot
26-27	pink palm	glove
28-29	giant butterfly	pen

Marcy and the competitors.
Did you see Marcy, sneaking around on almost every double page? And did you spot all the children on their way to the kite competition? How many children did you recognize on pages 28-29?

First published in 1995 by Usborne Publishing Ltd, Usborne House, 83-85 Saffron Hill, London EC1N 8RT, England.

Copyright © 1995 Usborne Publishing Ltd.

Printed in Portugal

First published in America August 1995.   UE

PUZZLE JUNGLE

Susannah Leigh

Illustrated by Brenda Haw

Contents

Series Editor: Gaby Waters
Assistant Editor: Michelle Bates
Layout: Nick Stone

About this book

This book is about James and Cath and their adventures in Puzzle Jungle. There are puzzles to solve on every double page. If you get stuck, you can look at the answers on pages 31 and 32.

Cath

James

Max

James and Cath are going to visit their friend Max, who lives in Puzzle Jungle. Max has written them a postcard. Here it is.

Puzzle Jungle
Tuesday

Dear James and Cath,
I can't wait for you to come and stay. I'll meet you at my treehouse on Friday. It's the one with the green door, remember?

Love Max
P.S Don't forget your kites!

James and Cath Cator

The Round House

Puzzle Town

Every year in Puzzle Jungle there is a spectacular kite flying competition. Children from all over the world come to take part. The kite that flies the highest is the winner. This year, James, Cath and Max are going to enter the competition.

2